MAXIMIZE YOUR HAPPINESS AND SUCCESS

By Leveraging Powerful Life Tools

ELISE MANCUSI AND BILL MANCUSI

outskirts
press

Introduction

THE FOLLOWING IS Bill's story of what led him to coauthor this book.

I was born in the 1960s and grew up in a suburb of Queens, New York. I lived in a second-floor apartment of a home with my parents and two sisters. My aunt and her four children lived in the first-floor apartment.

We lived a good life despite our environment being very challenging. We dealt with racial tension, crime, and economic challenges. We did our best to be positive and caring people.

I struggled to be happy. When taking on life's many difficult challenges, I routinely felt overwhelmed and discouraged. I would emotionally overreact to life's challenges instead of responding calmly, using my logic and intellect.

My reactions were emotional and physical sledgehammers. I chose to crush obstacles in my path. I would go into a fight mode and use physical or verbal assaults to resolve issues. This caused my life to be like a roller-coaster ride of emotional highs and lows.

Anxiety, fear, and depression entered my daily life. Feeling consistently happy seemed impossible. I could not see any light at the end of the tunnel.

In my later teens, I struggled making the transition to adulthood. I felt emotionally unstable and depressed.

Determined to improve my life, I began to research and observe various techniques used by highly successful people. These people included clergy, politicians, business professionals, family members, and friends. I observed that successful people leveraged techniques that gave them greater success.

I call these techniques *life tools*. I define life tools as various techniques that allow you to deal with life challenges more effectively.

I have also observed that highly successful people understand the importance of working outside of their comfort zone.

A comfort zone is where you embrace familiar and low-stress people, situations, and places. This is where you feel safest and have minimal risk.

When you embrace working routinely outside of your comfort zone, you will start to experience the following benefits:

- Greater opportunities.
- Development of new skills.
- Professional and personal growth.
- Greater productivity.
- Expanded network.
- Greater sense of value.

As I mentioned previously, my life tools of choice were emotional and physical sledgehammers. I would aggressively force results and crush obstacles.

This approach worked initially. But the results were not long lasting. On my journey of self-exploration, I was forced to realize the scary reality that these life tools were hurting my happiness and success. I needed to retire these tools and obtain a set of far more effective ones.

I continued my research and compiled a detailed list of highly effective life tools. I then refined each tool based on my own life experiences and packaged them in a friendly and easy-to-read format.

As I applied these life tools, I steadily began to see positive results. I was able to navigate demanding situations with greater ease and success than ever before. My anxiety, fear, and depression began to lessen. I began to project focused, confident, and calm energy to others on a more consistent basis.

My overall level of happiness and success was increasing with less effort than ever before. I became experienced in selecting the correct life tools to leverage for a given challenge. I learned to incorporate life tools and working outside my comfort zone into my daily life.

Incorporating Life Tools

When incorporating life tools, it is important to look beneath the surface of our unconscious mind at our beliefs and values.

These beliefs and values drive our behavior and overall results. You must be willing to explore and refine these beliefs and values. Refining our beliefs and values will change your behaviors and results.

When leveraging life tools, you start to feel more confident in yourself and the people around you. You learn not to resist but to enjoy and dance with life's challenges. The tougher life's challenges become, the more you need to embrace them spiritually, emotionally, and physically. Life tools help you accomplish this in the same manner that tools enable construction workers to manage difficult work-related challenges more effectively.

Walking through the journey of life with effective life tools enables us to feel more confident and competent.

As my confidence in the positive results of these tools grew, I began to share them with my teenage daughter, Elise. We would spend twenty to thirty minutes each evening discussing these tools and how she could apply them in addressing her life's challenges. I was amazed with the positive changes I saw in Elise. She displayed much more happiness, confidence, and focus. She soon began to share these tools with her close friends.

Sharing My Tools

Once these life tools were refined and documented, I began to provide private coaching and motivational classes on this material. My clients reported positive feedback. Many noted dramatic positive changes in their lives.

Now over thirty years later, I have decided to coauthor this book with my daughter Elise. Elise and I have worked together for the past two years on refining these life tools and writing this book.

The goal of this book is to help a much larger audience achieve greater happiness and success.

This book describes the many important life tools that I have learned. These life tools have enabled me to build a more solid personal foundation that allowed me to embrace life's many challenges more effectively.

NLP Exercises

This book leverages neurolinguistic programming (NLP) to help incorporate life tools into your unconscious mind.

NLP is a technique created in the 1970s. This technique claims that the NLP methodology can "model" the skills of exceptional people, allowing anyone to acquire those skills.

Corporations use NLP in their advertisements to sell their products. A famous hamburger chain in the early 1970s would have advertisements showing families happy and laughing while eating at their restaurants. These advertisements would begin to program unconscious minds to relate happiness with eating at this restaurant chain.

NLP has been adopted by many hypnotherapists and motivational speakers to provide leadership and peak performance training to businesses and government agencies.

Example of a NLP exercise for health:

- Every day in every way, I understand that I have only one physical body to transport me through life.
- Every day in every way, I understand that an unhealthy physical body is limited in its abilities.
- Every day in every way, I understand that a healthy physical body will increase happiness and minimize my depression and anxiety.
- Every day in every way, I will prioritize making healthy investments in my physical body.
- Every day in every way, I will feel happy, strong, grounded, and confident when I make healthy investments in my physical body.
- Every day in every way, I will make healthy eating and exercise a priority.
- Every day in every way, I will enjoy the many benefits of a healthy body.
- Every day in every way, I am in the driver's seat of life ensuring that I am making positive investments in my physical body.
- Every day in every way, I will feel healthy, loved, appreciated, and confident.

The following pages will open our toolbox and review in detail each of these life tools.

Life Tool of Personal Leadership

THE LIFE TOOL of personal leadership made a major positive impact in my life. It helped me feel strong, empowered, and in control.

Prior to understanding this tool, I would passively accept or consider myself a victim of what life throws my way. I was easily overwhelmed and extremely emotional.

This tool taught me to take charge of my life and acknowledge that I am not a victim.

What Is Personal Leadership?

Personal leadership is a state of mind in which you take control of your behavior and emotions in a way that will provide greater happiness and success.

You are now firmly in the driver's seat of life directing your destiny.

This does not mean that you will always get the outcome that you want. This means that you will not let others deter you from working toward your goals.

It is highly important to learn to accept and enjoy the feelings of nervousness and uncertainty. Embrace these feelings as a wonderful sign that you are working out of your comfort zone. Major positive changes happen when you are out of your comfort zone.

You will soon begin to realize that emotions cloud your vision. That *logic* and *intellect* should be your primary drivers when managing life challenges.

You will visualize that your logic and intellect are directly in front of your eyes and that your emotions are in your peripheral vision. You are still aware of your emotions, but they are not your main drivers.

You strongly believe in and defend your personal self-worth. You will not allow anyone to minimize your self-worth.

You will get a wonderful, confident, and satisfying feeling of ownership of your life.

You will recognize the strength derived from personal leadership.

You will understand that life is not a straight path. It is filled with unexpected detours. Appreciate these detours as life challenges that will make you even stronger.

You will embrace and dance with life's challenges. You will not resist them.

Here are a few very important rules to follow:

The 80–20 rule #1—80 percent of how you live your life is determined by your thoughts, and you reserve only 20 percent for the insight of others.

The 80–20 rule #2—80 percent of how you rate your level of happiness and success is determined by your thoughts, and you reserve only 20 percent for the insight of others.

Note: If you apply the reverse, the 20–80 percent rule, your life will be like an out-of-control emotional roller coaster. Others are directing your future.

Your happiness and success in life is not about luck! It is about managed thoughts, focused attention, and deliberate actions. You are directing your future.

Make personal leadership a major daily part of your life.

NLP Exercise for Personal Leadership:

- Every day in every way, I will activate personal leadership in my life.
- Every day in every way, I will be in the driver's seat of life directing my destiny.
- Every day in every way, I will understand that emotions cloud your vision.
- Every day in every way, I will leverage my logic and intellect as my primary drivers when managing life challenges.
- Every day in every way, I will not view myself as a victim.
- Every day in every way, 80 percent of how I live my life is determined by my thoughts and I reserve only 20 percent for the insight of others.
- Every day in every way, 80 percent of how I rate my level of happiness and success is determined by my thoughts and I reserve only 20 percent for the insight of others.
- Every day in every way, I will learn to accept and enjoy the feelings of nervousness and uncertainty as a sign that I am working out of my comfort zone!
- Every day in every way, I believe that major positive changes happen when I am out of my comfort zone.
- Every day in every way, I will guide my destiny.
- Every day in every way, I will lead, not follow.
- Every day in every way, I will be an amazing role model for the people around me.
- Every day in every way, I will enjoy life's journey as I work outside my comfort zone and leverage life tools.

Life Tool of a Balanced Personal Foundation

A BALANCED MIND creates a balanced personal foundation. A person with a balanced personal foundation can more effectively address the many challenges of life. Maintaining a balanced personal foundation is critical to long-lasting happiness and success.

Prior to learning this tool, I would obsess on one aspect of my life and neglect others. This negatively impacted my marriage, family, work, and health. I now make daily positive investments in six important aspects of my life. As I incorporated this tool in my daily life, my happiness and success improved greatly.

What Is a Balanced Personal Foundation?

Builders know the importance of establishing a solid and balanced foundation before a structure is built. A home with a solid and balanced foundation can better endure harsh conditions.

Let's explore the example of two cargo ships traveling through rough waters. The captain of the first cargo ship wants to set sail quickly and instructs his crew to randomly place cargo in the ship. This makes the ship unbalanced. The captain of the second cargo ship instructs his crew to carefully place cargo in the ship based on weight and ensure that the cargo is well balanced. As the two ships sail toward their destination, they encounter a powerful storm generating high waves. The first ship is unable to manage the storm and must slow down and change course to avoid sinking. The unbalanced cargo causes the ship to rock wildly and take on substantial amounts of water. The second ship can manage the storm and stay on course toward its destination.

The lesson to learn here is that life will present you with challenges or "waves," but a balanced person will handle these challenges more effectively and will be able to stay on course.

A strong personal foundation allows you to deal with life's challenges like water rolling off a duck's back. Minimal effect.

Ensuring that every day is balanced with busy activities will reduce the impact of anxiety, fear, and depression in your life.

To build a strong and balanced personal foundation, you will need to make *strong, positive daily* investments in the following six key aspects of life.

Aspect of Life	Description
Spirituality	Daily spiritual awareness of one's inner beliefs and values. This includes practicing a formal religion.
Health	Daily investment in your emotional and physical well-being. This includes being physically and emotionally fit.
Partner	Daily investment in improving your current relationship or looking for your soul mate.
Family	Daily investment in quality time with family members.
Friends	Daily investment in quality time with friends.
Work	Daily investment in earning income, attending school, completing chores, and managing savings.

Making strong positive daily investments into these six key aspects of your life will strengthen your personal foundation and enhance your ability to manage life's challenges.

You will leverage a positive, confident, calm, assertive, and humble state of mind when making these investments.

It is extremely helpful to keep a daily tracker of your positive investments in the six key life aspects.

Example of a daily tracker:

Life Aspects	1/1/23
Spirituality	Go to church, pray, and read spiritual books.
Health	Exercise, eat healthy, and go to counseling.
Partner	Discuss today's events and life's challenges.
Family	Help your children with their homework.
Friends	Call a friend.
Work	Focus on your assigned work tasks.

Sharing this tracker with a trusted person will make you more accountable.

Remember, always stay balanced!

NLP Exercise for a Balanced Personal Foundation:

- Every day in every way, I will acknowledge that a balanced personal foundation is critical to lasting happiness and success.
- Every day in every way, I will make strong positive investments in the six aspects of my life: spirituality, health, partner, family, friends, and work.
- Every day in every way, I will acknowledge that investing in these six aspects of my life will reduce the impact of anxiety, fear, and depression.
- Every day in every way, I will acknowledge that a balanced personal foundation allows me to deal with life's challenges like water rolling off a duck's back. Minimal effect.
- Every day in every way, I will enjoy life's journey as I work outside my comfort zone and leverage life tools.

Life Tool of Surrendering the Outcome

PRIOR TO LEARNING this tool, a major part of my time was spent worrying about failed outcomes. These outcomes included world affairs, work, family, friends, and health.

This overwhelming fear would consume my thoughts and minimize my ability to focus on enjoying the journey and accomplishing my goals. Fear, anxiety, and depression would begin to flourish!

What is Surrending the Outcome?

I observed that highly effective people focus on their personal performance and the quality of their work. They accept that the outcome is beyond their direct control. They do not worry about failures or a negative outcome. They have learned that the fear of failure will consume them and minimize their level of happiness and success.

It is essential to direct all of your mind, body, and soul toward obtainable goals.

Find happiness and joy in every aspect of your life.

Surround yourself with positive thinking people who are also focused on obtainable goals. Avoid negative and doomsday thinking people.

This includes all forms of media. Media can bombard you with negative and damaging content that feeds fear, anxiety, and depression.

Upon incorporating this tool into my life, I changed how I focused on life challenges.

I now live my life with the following approach:

- Filter out or minimize life challenges that I cannot change.
- Focus on the effort required to resolve life challenges that I can change.
- Assess situations with logic and intellect. Leave emotions to the side. Emotions will cloud your vision.
- Embrace and dance with life's journey.
- Enjoy life's journey.
- Embrace all outcomes.
- Embrace failures as steppingstones to happiness and success.
- Find the good in all outcomes.
- Spread love and positive energy to all aspects of my life.

Work hard every day to live the above approach.

Some days will be easier than others.

Surrendering the outcome greatly increases your happiness, inner peace, confidence, and focus.

NLP Exercise for Surrendering the Outcome:

- Every day in every way, I will focus on my personal performance.
- Every day in every way, I will focus on the quality of my work.
- Every day in every way, I will accept that the outcome is beyond my direct control.
- Every day in every way, I will love and appreciate my many strengths.
- Every day in every way, I will embrace life's journey.
- Every day in every way, I will enjoy life's journey.
- Every day in every way, I will embrace all outcomes.
- Every day in every way, I will embrace failures as steppingstones to happiness and success.
- Every day in every way, I will see the good in all outcomes!
- Every day in every way, I will feel strong love and appreciation for the people in my life.
- Every day in every way, I will strongly believe in myself and my abilities.
- Every day in every way, I will smile when I encounter negative feedback and energy.
- Every day in every way, I will enjoy life's journey as I work outside my comfort zone and leverage life tools.

Life Tool of the Fence of Life

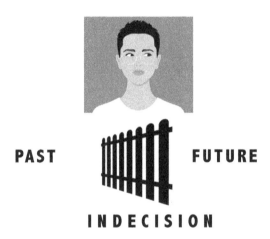

PAST **FUTURE**

INDECISION

What is the Fence of Life?

WHEN YOU ARE resting on the fence of life, you are embracing indecision. You are holding on to the past and not fully embracing the future. You create stories justifying your lack of action.

You need to honestly assess each situation and determine if you are resting in indecision on the fence of life. This can be particularly challenging during emotional situations. An honest assessment is critical for lasting happiness and success.

You need to strongly believe that prolonged periods of indecision will minimize your happiness and success. You need to confidently embrace and move toward the future.

Prior to understanding this tool, I would delay progress and change for extended periods of time. I would hold on to the past being afraid to move forward. This was the root cause of many lost opportunities. This was evident during a painful divorce. I was in limbo for over eight years. This was not healthy for me or my daughter.

This tool reshaped my life. I now embrace positive change and understand the harm of indecision. I am much more comfortable with change and letting go of the past. Change is still difficult at times, but I now understand the danger with extended periods of indecision.

You are most vulnerable when you linger on the fence of life.

NLP Exercise for Fence of Life:

- Every day in every way, I will not linger in indecision on the fence of life.
- Every day in every way, I will not hold on to the past.
- Every day in every way, I will confidently embrace and move toward the future.
- Every day in every way, I will embrace life's journey.
- Every day in every way, I will enjoy life's journey as I work outside my comfort zone and leverage life tools.

Life Tool of Effective Personal Energy

THIS TOOL WAS a major game changer for me. Before learning about this tool, I was not aware that people projected energy. I thought people just spoke words.

As I learned and applied this tool, I could see people responding to me in a far more positive manner. I gained far more cooperation, motivation, and loyalty from the people around me. This allowed me greater happiness and success.

What Is Personal Energy?

All living things project personal energy to each other. This energy is a major part of how living things communicate. Personal energy is a combination of many factors.

These factors include the following:

- Spiritual beliefs.
- Past experiences.
- Current situation.
- Fearful thoughts.
- Dominant thoughts.
- Passive thoughts.

The energy that you project has an impact on your state of mind and the people around you. Your energy can either have a positive or negative impact on a situation.

The following emotional states contribute to effective energy:

- Welcoming.
- Positive.
- Supportive.
- Desire for win-win outcomes. (Everyone wins)
- Respectful.
- Humbleness.
- Calmness.
- Confidence.
- Patience.
- Assertiveness.

When projecting energy to others, visualize and incorporate the above emotional states.

Remove the following negative emotional states from your projected energy:

- Unwelcoming.
- Negative.
- Uncooperative.
- Desire for win-lose outcomes. (You win and someone loses)
- Disrespectful.
- Arrogance.
- Nervousness.
- Emotional.
- Jealousy.
- Insecurity.
- Aggressiveness.
- Fearfulness.
- Victim mentality.

Levels of energy:

It is also important to choose the correct level of energy that you project.

Projected energy is categorized in the following zones:

Red Zone	Projects extremely high, unfocused, and hostile energy (Fight mode)
Yellow Zone	Projects moderately high, focused, and nonhostile energy. (Determined)
Green Zone	Projects low, focused, and welcoming energy (Open to discuss)

The *green and yellow zones* are highly effective for most situations.

People perceive others by their projected energy.

NLP Exercise for Effective Personal Energy:

- Every day in every way, I will project positive energy.
- Every day in every way, I will visualize and incorporate positive emotional states when projecting energy to others.
- Every day in every way, I will project strong and confident energy.
- Every day in every way, I will avoid the red zone.
- Every day in every way, I will not view myself as a victim.
- Every day in every way, I will feel strong love and appreciation for the people in my life.
- Every day in every way, I will smile when I encounter negative feedback and energy.
- Every day in every way, I will enjoy the journey.
- Every day in every way, I will spread love and positive energy to all aspects of my life.
- Every day in every way, I will enjoy life's journey as I work outside my comfort zone and leverage life tools.

Life Tool of Planning

I OBSERVED THAT most successful people do detailed planning prior to working toward a goal.

This was the opposite of my approach. I thought I was such a strong leader that I never needed to plan. I would just jump into action. I would figure things out as I went along. The reality is that my approach made the work more difficult and increased mistakes that impacted my efforts. Often, these unnecessary mistakes caused me to lose credibility with others.

When I finally made the decision to incorporate planning in my life, it allowed me to organize, prioritize, visualize, and track my tasks and overall progress toward my goals. I found myself less emotionally reactive when obstacles entered my path. My thoughts remain logical and focused. My level of confidence and calmness increased with each passing day. People commented that I appeared more focused and organized.

My happiness and success took a major positive leap when I implemented planning into my daily life. I am just sorry that I did not embrace planning much sooner.

What Is Planning?

Planning allows you to organize and track the tasks required to accomplish a goal. Planning improves your ability to visualize and manage your work and time. *You now look at goals as a series of small tasks.*

For proper planning, you will need to create written plans. A written plan is a step-by-step list of tasks required to accomplish a goal.

It is important to create plans for both your daily goals and your long-term goals. Goals need to be clearly defined with realistic deadlines. Any delays or issues should be resolved promptly.

Create and print out your long-term plans. Check off each task once completed. Revise the task list as needed.

Example of a long-term plan:

6/22 - Review your budget to determine a monthly car payment that you can afford.

7/11 - Confirm with five banks the current interest rates and your credit approval.

7/15 - Decide what type of vehicle you want. SUV was selected.

7/22 - Research various SUV models within your budget.

8/11 - Go to various dealerships and look at selected cars.

8/11 - Test drive several cars.

8/15 - Select the car.

8/15 - Negotiate the price.

8/16 - Obtain financing.

8/17 - Obtain insurance.

8/18 - Purchase the car.

Create and print out your daily plan each day. Check off each task once completed. Revise the task list as needed.

Example of a daily plan:

8:00 a.m. - Walk the dog.

8:30 a.m. - Take my daughter to school.

9:00 a.m. - Refuel the car.

9:30 a.m. - Clean the house.

12:00 p.m. - Walk the dog.

12:30 p.m. - Feed the dog.

1:00 p.m. - Pay bills.

2:00 p.m. - Pick up my daughter from school.

4:00 p.m. - Review my daughter's homework.

5:00 p.m. - Cook dinner.

6:00 p.m. - Prepare dinner for my daughter.

7:00 p.m. - Walk the dog.

9:00 p.m. - Say prayers.

Always remember:

When you plan, you plan to succeed.

When you do not plan, you plan to fail.

NLP Exercise for Planning:

- Every day in every way, when I plan, I will plan to succeed.
- Every day in every way, I will embrace planning for short-term goals.
- Every day in every way, I will embrace planning long-term goals.
- Every day in every way, I will feel focused, calm, positive, and assertive when I plan.
- Every day in every way, I will feel strong love and appreciation for the people in my life.
- Every day in every way, I will smile when I encounter project delays.
- Every day in every way, I will enjoy life's journey as I work outside my comfort zone and leverage life tools.

Life Tool of Teamwork

ADDING TEAMWORK TO my daily life reduced my anxiety and stress. I was not alone. I was part of a team sharing the challenge. This team environment was very calming and motivating.

What Is Teamwork?

Teamwork is the activity of working together in a focused, positive, and cooperative manner with other people. It is the understanding that team members are working for each other.

Managing life's challenges when you are a member of a strong team is much more effective than working alone. You need to learn how to embrace teamwork with shared goals and victories. You need to foster team-building behaviors. Do not isolate yourself when working on difficult challenges. Leverage the power of a team.

Your team members should include other great people who can do the following:

- Illuminate your path to success.
- Push you to dig deeper and accomplish more.
- Share your goals.
- Make you happy.
- Make you laugh.

- Make you feel good about yourself.
- Show your support even in tough times.
- Enable you to lead, not follow.

These are the people who will help you achieve lasting happiness and success.

NLP Exercise for Teamwork:

- Every day in every way, I will incorporate teamwork into my life.
- Every day in every way, teamwork will make me feel calm, confident, and focused.
- Every day in every way, I will embrace planning long-term goals.
- Every day in every way, I will embrace planning short-term goals.
- Every day in every way, I will feel strong love and appreciation for the people in my life.
- Every day in every way, I will enjoy life's journey as I work outside my comfort zone and leverage life tools.

Life Tool of Educated Risk-Taking

LASTING SUCCESS IS highly impacted by embracing educated risks. You need to analyze pending risks and determine if the risk vs. reward is positive or negative.

Educated risks empowered me to take on more challenges with greater success. I better understood whether the risk was worth the potential rewards. This made me more confident and assertive.

What Is Educated Risk-Taking?

Embracing risks with a positive risk vs. reward is critical to achieving happiness and success.

An educated risk requires the following due diligence:

- A detailed review of the pros and cons of taking this risk.
- A detailed assessment of the return on investment of taking this risk (what can you gain and what can you lose).
- If the return on investment is positive, consider taking this risk.

The tool of educated risk-taking teaches you the following concepts:

- Embrace educated risk.
- Embrace educated failures as steppingstones to remarkable success.
- Smile and learn from educated failures.
- Educated failures are positive events.
- Understand that fear of failure is unhealthy.
- Understand that educated failures are healthy.
- Do not let fear of failure consume you.

Failures are the steppingstones to remarkable success.

You always want a positive return on your investments.

Examples of risk:

#1—Leave my current secure job for a new job with greater compensation and advancement. Sounds like a positive risk versus reward. This risk makes sense.

#2—Leave my current secure job at sixty years old to train as an Olympic runner. Currently the sole provider for a family of five. Sounds like a negative risk versus reward. This risk does not make sense.

Embrace risks with positive risks vs. rewards.

NLP Exercise for Educated Risk-Taking:

- Every day in every way, I will embrace educated risk-taking.
- Every day in every way, I will accept challenges with a positive risk vs. reward.
- Every day in every way, I will not let fear of failure consume me.
- Every day in every way, I will acknowledge that educated failures are the steppingstones to great success.
- Every day in every way, I will feel strong love and appreciation for the people in my life.
- Every day in every way, I will enjoy life's journey as I work outside my comfort zone and leverage life tools.

Life Tool of Coping Skills

THE LIFE TOOL of coping skills consists of the positive actions that we take to deal with stressful, challenging, and uncomfortable situations.

Prior to learning this tool, I struggled to respond to unexpected challenges. I internalized my feelings and this emotionally clouded my thoughts.

This life tool provided me with a list of coping skills that allowed me to respond to life's challenges in a more effective manner. As I incorporated this tool in my daily life, I became more stable and effective.

What Are Coping Skills?

Coping skills affect how you respond to life's challenges. Positive coping skills are a major contributor to lasting happiness and success.

Examples of positive coping skills:

- Do not take situations too seriously.
- Smile and laugh about the situation.
- De-escalate the situation.
- Enjoy the journey.

- Take time to think about the situation before responding.
- Evaluate all sides of the situation before responding.
- Look for winning outcomes for everyone involved.
- Guide your responses primarily by logic and intellect. Leave emotions to the side.
- Exercise to relax your mind.
- View everyone involved in the situation as being on the same side.
- Appreciate and focus on the good in all situations.
- Interject compassion in responding to a situation.
- View the situation as a discussion, not a conflict.
- Use calm, confident, positive, focused, and assertive energy.
- Believe that everyone involved is working toward a positive outcome from their perspective.

It is critical to your happiness and success that you consistently use positive coping skills.

It is also critical to your happiness and success that you avoid negative coping skills.

Examples of negative coping skills:

- Avoiding the situation or running away.
- Becoming highly emotional.
- Becoming aggressive or hostile (verbally or physically).
- Allowing fear and anger to consume you.
- Allowing nervous energy to guide you.
- Being excessively dependent emotionally on another person.
- Self-medicating with excessive food, alcohol, smoking, sleeping, spending, or drugs.

Embrace positive coping skills

Avoid negative coping skills

NLP Exercise for Coping Skills:

- Every day in every way, I will embrace positive coping skills.
- Every day in every way, I will avoid negative coping skills.
- Every day in every way, I will acknowledge that positive coping skills are a major contributor to lasting happiness and success.
- Every day in every way, I will not let fear of failure consume me.
- Every day in every way, I will feel strong love and appreciation for the people in my life.
- Every day in every way, I will enjoy life's journey as I work outside my comfort zone and leverage life tools.

Life Tool of Healthy Boundaries

DEFINING AND ENFORCING healthy boundaries is an important part of establishing your individual identity, achieving happiness, and achieving success.

What are Healthy Boundaries?

- A boundary is a limit or space between you and other people. This space may be physical or emotional.
- A boundary defines where your personal space begins and ends.
- A boundary guides other people as to what space they can enter.
- Boundaries are an important part of mental health and well-being.
- Healthy boundaries help you define your individuality.
- A lack of healthy boundaries may indicate that you do not have a strong self-identity or are entangled with the identity of others.
- Healthy boundaries are those boundaries that are set to make sure you are stable emotionally and physically.

Healthy Boundary Guidelines:

- Find happiness and peace within yourself.
- Do not seek to be highly significant to others.
- Embrace and accept any level of significance in the lives of others.
- Do not monopolize conversations. Be a great listener.

- Confidently and clearly define and enforce your emotional and physical boundaries.
- Limit deep emotional sharing to professionals, close family members, and longtime friends.
- Respect others' personal space, time, and privacy.
- Avoid stalking-like behavior; limit calling or texting.

NLP Exercise for Healthy Boundaries:

- Every day in every way, I will define and enforce healthy boundaries.
- Every day in every way, I will acknowledge that healthy boundaries help ensure that I am stable emotionally and physically.
- Every day in every way, I will feel strong love and appreciation for the people in my life.
- Every day in every way, I will enjoy life's journey as I work outside my comfort zone and leverage life tools.

Working This Program

REPETITION IS CRITICAL to the success of this program. The more you read about and apply these life tools, the more effective you will become.

It is also extremely helpful to share and discuss this program with others.

Program Steps:

- Commit to one fifty-minute session each week.
- During each session, listen to relaxing music and minimize interruptions.
- Each session will consist of the following:
    - » o Begin the session with five minutes of upper body stretching and deep breaths.
    - » o Next take forty minutes to review each life tool and the associated NLP exercise.
    - » o Next take five minutes to visualize how you would apply these life tools to existing or pending life challenges to maximize your happiness and success.
- Every day apply the following to your life:
    - » o Remember to love and appreciate the people and places around you.
    - » o Leverage your logic and intellect.
    - » o Strive for win-win outcomes!

Conclusion

THIS BOOK PROVIDES a toolbox full of valuable life tools. You must now take the time to follow this program and learn how to effectively leverage them.

Remember, life is extremely challenging with many obstacles jumping in our path.

These life tools will enable you to overcome more obstacles than ever before with greater happiness and success. You will most likely need to retire some of your existing life tools!

It is critical that you strive to enjoy life's journey as you work outside your comfort zone and leverage these life tools.

Several Key Points to Remember:

- This program is not about being perfect.
- This program is not about judging others.
- This program is about learning how to apply a set of effective life tools to maximize your happiness and success.

Congratulations on beginning this important journey.

Printed in the USA
CPSIA information can be obtained
at www.ICGtesting.com
LVHW091515300923
759526LV00006B/1434